G & S

Ghazals and Sonnets in Conversation

G & S

Ghazals and Sonnets in Conversation

Tric O'Heare and Ross Donlon

Cover image | Ross Donlon

ISBN 9781763653092

Walleah Press
South Launceston
Tasmania, Australia 7249

www.walleahpress.com.au
ralph.wessman@walleahpress.com.au

G & S

Ghazals and Sonnets in Conversation

Ross Donlon & Tric O'Heare

Contents

Dreaming Awake

Before an open window and the night's silhouette of trees, dreaming awake,
a cool touch arrives like a guest as if something else is near, dreaming awake.

So perhaps the old maps are right, and somewhere a face with streaming hair
has sent a breath in kinship, caressing the mind while we're dreaming awake.

Half inside time's looking glass, half beneath a Plimsoll line of consciousness,
the heart counts in a cave dark with hope, fear and longing, dreaming awake.

Five senses explore five ways of staying alive, while the sixth and coxswain,
directs a pulse each night of the year, rowing night into day, dreaming awake.

After eighty orbits through the firmament, patrolling dark and light,
these six pull me ashore each day and I rise. Until then, I'm dreaming awake.

Waking the Island

We wake the island when we clear it of weeds.
For two generations of dreams, it slept
under the blackberry, thistles, and reeds.
A secret that the quiet creek kept.
An old woman begged us to *leave be*
the willow anchoring it to the creek bed,
pleading its evergreenesss in the heat,
urging us to ignore its foreignness,
to believe how beloved it was of the mare
she swam upstream on high summer days
and tethered in the shade it cast there
while she herself lay dreaming, awake,
that nothing would change, they would always be
the same girl, horse, island, and weeping tree.

The Days of Horses

Grandfather lived his week for the days of horses.
I cut them from papers on a floor of torn horses.

He'd be propped up in bed, Old Man Mountain God
crumpled as form guides and sports pages of horses.

Linoleum stretched a green course around the room.
A mirror reflected the game of looking glass horses.

The radio sang its minaret song all Saturday long.
Race callers cried the ghost names of invisible horses.

A door suddenly opened could blow the field like fate,
skew the race. Paper shadows forgot they were horses.

God-in-bed rocked the springs. *Six to Four th' Field!*
Two to One Bar One! Bookies cheered for his lost horses.

Each call's word play made the state of races a mystery
but chanting drummed the coming of galloping horses:

Rising Fast Tim Whiffler The Grafter White Nose Carbine
Comic Court Peter Pan Spearfelt: a wordspell of horses.

Around and around they swept through my childhood,
first spoken word poems heard from the naming of horses

The Hunt

Rockpools in shelves that rim the harbour
endlessly re-enact beginnings of life,
elemental models of how to start
a world, how to hunt or wait, flee or hide.
At the water surface, an insect throws
tiny shadows of its moving feet
onto the sandy floor far below,
six dark dots, a code that is hard to read.
For the bug whose weight water will not bear,
it means slow death. She is destined
to become a water strider's dinner,
playing out a role, as does her assassin.
Nearby, lions have escaped their enclosure
and concerned helicopters circle, then hover.

Scenes of Sydney

By night, Sydney harbour is encircled by a coronet of diamonds.
Wave crests fleck blue to white, slashed and star-cut by diamonds.

These might be ferries or other busy shipping, moored or moving.
High-rise towers of the rich shimmer reflections of glittering diamonds.

Sydney can be a hard town. Kings Cross lends its name to metaphor
easily. It's hard to turn right. In the gutters, chips of moonlit diamonds.

On endless nights old streets obey colonial mapmakers, curve above
indigenous streams and gullies to the Tank Stream's hidden diamonds.

Each day the traffic snakes in, shedding skin to the hammers of breakfast
jocks. Rail commuters wake to the roar of metal and sun-blazed diamonds.

Beyond Sydney, outer suburbs hedge their bets and look to the mountains.
Postcard swims are far away. In winter, rugby flags of bristling diamonds.

Explorers' trails from Parramatta River turned scrub into a suburb. Ashfield.
Arising from terra cotta, *Peek Frean's* biscuit factory. Its scent of diamonds.

I spent my youth there, anxious to get to the harbour where life real began
(I thought) anywhere East of West, callow with my rough cut diamonds

Placeholder

What is it that you would lend your name to?
A star? A thimble-sized orchid? A hall?
The sense that someone is looking for you?
That feeling you get as you start to fall?
Is it to regret that you'd give your name?
The ancient gesture you would not make?
The glass too few, the missed kiss, unfair blame,
the swim in the ocean you would not take?
There are places you have already lent it:
inside those books you want others to like,
on the donor card that offers your 'bits',
and beneath the poems you had to write.
Place holder. Ephemera. The name you go by.
Rejoice, you are lucky. It has lasted a lifetime.

Twilight

The dead are invisible, they are not absent.
St Augustine.

It's twilight here but perhaps for you still night
my love, writing your poem of grief each night.

Your bedroom will be dark, all windows locked,
curtains drawn to block out light. Rescue night.

The house is wound around your heart in a maze.
Only you know where threads lie strewn at night.

Your nightgown, your 'gown of night', white lace
patterned in tiny stars, is a pale blue ghost at night.

Perhaps for now you live in reflection, day bright
with illusion, grieving in lieu of sleep each night.

Day revives memory, the shock of sudden loss.
I wait til sunlight dies, watch over you by night.

I remember pale shoulders turning from me
like the moon's last phase, the purity of night.

Even here, time passes. Sorrow, like moonlight,
grows then fades, but love is constant as night.

Spells From the Universe

On clear, still nights, the moon and stars are real.
No clouds move gauzily between them and us
to make us question what we can see.
Heroes, sisters, a saucepan or a cross,
our familiar things are out there in the dark,
yet this is the time of imminence too.
The urgent gap between a distant dog's barks.
Pre-storm, pre-dawn, pre-turning towards you.
Such nights are spells from the universe.
Respite from hope, doubt and memory.
Suspension of time. Thought ellipsis.
No need for analysis or augury.
Earth has not yet tipped us into our next day.
Nothing is too early, nothing too late.

'We have heard the chimes at midnight'

Falstaff, from *Henry IV*

The hardest chimes to hear are those which strike at midnight,
a sound when time ends time. Bells toll the death of midnight.

The heart rides each echo in the long, mourning cry of farewell.
Fear grows in every cell. Prayers try to stay alive at midnight.

Doomed ones know how precious is time between each chime.
A longest day ends at twelve. The sky opens wide at midnight.

Wolf hour. Witching hour. Brightest stars are light years away.
Moonlight ebbs with the tide. Life blooms and dies at midnight.

Race the dawn. How much can a day hold? Dreams are nightmare.
Past is present. Shutting in, dark draws down the mind at midnight.

As an invisible procession passed, Antony knew his time had come.
Alexandria! Unearthly music as gods abandoned him at midnight.

Whatever minute our hearts break, convention provides one full day.
Penned, scratched or chiselled, record of death is always midnight.

Time watched as a young Queen knelt, fumbling at her blindfold.
Her women wept as History looked on, ready to strike at midnight.

Alignment

Let me tell you about the day you died.
I was washing dishes, wishing the water
got hotter quicker. While I held my hands
under the running tap I gazed down and saw
that once again I had taken off my ring
to keep it safe during my tree planting
and left it somewhere now unremembered.
I glanced up, trying to retrace my movements,
got distracted by the sight of young roos
play-fighting and then my eye was caught
by the rocky southern hills flaring white
as they aligned with the setting sun.
I was thinking I must climb those hills one day,
when, precisely then, my phone began to ring.

Radda

After two hours the bus climbs in and over hills from Florence to Radda,
a hilltop town in Chianti. Postcard romance is charmed by reality in Radda.

Amphitheatre sky, tiny pepper-pot town sustained by hills, once war fodder
between Florence and Sienna. Now their statues and vines lead you to Radda.

In Tuscan summers wild boars snuffle, root in ruins and woods. Ordered groves
rollercoast hills. The past is close as an Etruscan shard waiting for you in Radda.

At night, wilderness barks back at hills. Animals retake the dark as the moon
wakes villas, silvers pools. In a stone garden, horizons of towers guard Radda.

The sun leaps from a hill like a deer. Dawn surrounds with bird sound. Cockerels
wake cars, then cafes. But dusk is slow to leave. Drinks gleam on a terrace in Radda.

Hills approach and recede, a kind of time tide. Heat still rises from Roman stone.
Panna cotta soothes evenings on a terrace. Tomorrow's plans are stardust in Radda.

Memory, my restless ancestor, merges with the landscape. Familiarity and friends
beat the heart like a drum. Hills fit like a jigsaw, this unlikely piece at home in Radda.

Home

A girl stands at the end of a dirt road.
She rests one hand on top of a large case
that leans into her leg like a pet dog.
She is being watched from one pace behind
by an older woman in an apron.
The track they are on must lead to their home
in the mountains that are the island's spine.
In front of them is the south-north highway
which I am travelling on, in a bus
bound for the harbour. As we pass, I see
the women turn to each other and smile –
pleased that they will have more time together
because my bus has the wrong number for them.
There we still are, at the point of before.

Apron

My grandmother stands at the kitchen sink of our small flat wearing her favourite apron. Tied at the back, the loops too hard for a small boy to ignore. Granny knot of her apron.

Not bought but made. The singer pedal sewing machine rattles across cheap cotton cloth, edges hemmed with a vibrant match. Red rickrack braid trims her black and white apron.

Solitary at the sink, small statue in after-hours of washing, peeling, cooking, wiping and putting away. The long, grey, work skirt sways steps of a kitchen ritual. Solitary dance in a new apron.

Summer sunlight angles into the narrow window of the flat, turns sink suds into snowflakes. But heat beats the kitchen like a gong. Baking his baked dinner, grease stains on her apron.

Fireside, winter's kerosene heater, a cosy name with different connotations in small flat life. Tripping not allowed under spell of Dante's *Inferno*. Stable for a clothes horse drying her apron.

Family departed. Alone at last bereft, that family paradox. Children gone but left with his ghost. Daily teacup and saucer, best too fine for breaking. Breaking nonetheless. Falling from her apron.

A kind of hopscotch on the kitchen linoleum. Parkinson calls with respect. Short jumps into Hospital. Hospital. Hospital. Nursing Home. *Bed-ridden* - that odd phrase. Independence gone with her apron.

A protective garment worn over the front of one's clothes, tied at the back. (We all need protection). *From Old French. 'naperon'. The 'n' in 'naperon' lost by wrong division.* (Time will do that). Our apron.

Child point of view of an adult growing older. Nan's shanks narrow into worn slippers. Varicose veins bulge from a lifetime standing. I reach and undo the strings. Again, not looking up, she reties her apron.

Undoing

To learn to tie shoelaces is a rite
that most children readily pass through.
It is not the first of life's basic how-to's
but it is an important one to get right.
Other doing-ups will follow – we're taught
to button a shirt, seal a bag, cap a pen,
lock a cage, close a coop, tie an apron,
compose our faces and act unhurt.
And *un*doing seems easy when we're young.
One foot can bring down a castle in the sand.
A plait becomes just hair in newly deft hands.
Ice cream domes flatten under our tongues.
If we are lucky, it's a while before
we learn which things cannot be undone.

Caravan

We trail from the rented holiday house, a linked caravan
of past and present, desert travellers in a tinkling caravan.

Pop leads in shorts, Messiah in Persil-white singlet and skin
weathered as leather. His boots make prints for our caravan.

It's a trek for all ages. Hills climb past grey, fibro cottages
set in sand and heat. Sleepy snakes watch a clinking caravan.

My young mother carries a book and gay beach umbrella.
Nan follows with lunch, sandwiches and cold drinks caravan.

Cousin Amy and I tote buckets, spades, goggles and towels.
The sun floats egg-white, mirage of a flickering caravan.

After forever, sand dunes of a beach rise like the Sahara.
Tussocks shrink as time disappears from our shifting caravan.

Somewhere in and out of line, ghosts tramp weary headed,
merge then retire again to memory from a shrinking caravan.

The ocean appears, a sunken oasis. We slide down hills, thirsty
for its salty embrace. Waves roll in chains of a shimmering caravan:

originally from North Africa, Persia, Arabia, the Crusades' Old French
and Latin: *Company of travellers going together for security:* our caravan.

Here we are inside the paraphernalia of lunch in a typical post-war
holiday. Nan, Pop, Mum, my cousin and me, a time-blinkered caravan.

Walking back, the long day exhausted, my grandfather's heart pauses
to rest half way. *Margin's Orange Ice Cream* his treat for our caravan.

The day's trail disappears like Arabian Nights, broken by the spell of home
and shared meal with family, dimmed by the dream of a vanishing caravan.

The Isthmus

For Genevieve

At night we sneak out onto the isthmus
clutching each other, laughing quietly,
fearful of the dark and other people
in their shacks in the thicketing tea trees.
On the long beach we watch the mainland lights
until the littlest ones have almost all gone out
then use our cigarettes as pointers to the stars
making up an astronomy just for us.
No-one's lover yet. No-one's mother yet.
Our ponytails brush against our bare backs,
silver bells tinkle our ankles and wrists
when we shatter the foamy water's edge.
We walk the moon's path in the shallow sea
loving how it heals like a dream behind us.

We Ran Flying

It was a time when boys never knock but gather outside your flat, ready for flying.
Someone shouts to make you look & there wait Ric and Moose, revving for flying.

Dusk has begun. Night flows a draught over beds getting infants ready for sleep,
but adolescence flicks ignitions on the engines of us, an evening perfect for flying.

Footpaths become runways, street lights line a hilly tarmac as we ease into formation,
agree on a secret flight path across yesterday's suburb, starlit course cleared for flying.

Soaring into sky as sun sets, we rise higher as glare of day fades into its hanger
& night takes over, turning a training run for the school Aths. Carnival into flying.

Sixteen. Old enough to be 'let out at night', phrase reminiscent of something caged
released into air and we are, our sneakers become wings, aligned & primed for flying.

Above the disappearing streets and invisible roads we rise, sublime as gods on holiday.
Dusk becomes night, searchlights rove looking for boys/almost men/ still children/ flying.

Sixty years on in another flight through space, the sensation returns, a dream relived;
the weightless thrill of youth one summer evening lifting us from the future, free & flying.

A Friend Borrows my Madonna Icon

A friend borrows my Madonna icon.
Seed-pearl inserts. Paua shell inlay.
She says it's to base a self-portrait upon,
with herself centred, not looking away.
She covers a panel with fish glue, chalky white,
building a ground up, layer by layer
that will fire the work with an inner light
when sun penetrates the precious tempera.
Ochre for yellow. Cinnabar for red.
And lapis, the only stone that says, 'sky'.
Even gold for gold. No expense is spared
to give her image luminosity.
But instead of a halo of mother-of-pearl
she wears a crown incised, *Ordinary Girl.*

Madonna

Enter the boys-own-not-centre-page black and white photographs of Madonna
young naked porn limbs half open to the passive camera – playgirl Madonna.

First reference in *Firefox*. Google how you will. Start up your search engines
you'll only find Madge. Madonna Louise Ciciccone, *Queen of Pop* Madonna.

In the Beginning, the word rocks out of the Beatles' hit: *Baby at your breast, wonders
how you manage to feed the rest.* But wasn't she someone's one-time lady, *Madonna?*

In a sepulchre shop window, lines of plastic statues trademark the downcast eyes,
outstretched hands and piteous acceptance. Stereotypical import. China Madonna.

But somewhere in history she was fourteen, Joe her builder boy rather older.
Theologians and historians spin wheels of self-interest. But what's lost is Madonna.

Poor wee girl, swallowed by a god. Or gods. Transformed by blind fate and faith
into circus icon, Christmas card, Morning Star. But what about Mary, Madonna?

Next-to-central-figure in every nativity scene, each barn animal iconic, virgin
womb borrowed for immaculate conception. Christmas delivery. Blue Madonna.

Queen of Heaven with no King. *Mathew 1:19 Joseph, being a just man and not willing
to make her a public example, was minded to put her away privately,* His Ex. Madonna.

Spread below the cross like a blanket, the eyes uplift asking? But no answer there
from a gathering of grey clouds streaked with someone's heaven. *Pieta* Madonna.

Blue-cream plaster sorrowful statue in St Everywhere welcomes the poor and penitent,
Our Lady more working class sufferer than someone's martyr, a People's Madonna.

My mother's Go-To. Another woman who found trouble in war with men. Her
familiar face from childhood looking back sad, suffering and kind. My Madonna

On Being Seasick

Once I was seasick and tried to hide it.
Impossible on a small boat in a rough sea
with a French man, observant and kind.
Ma pauvre, tu as le mal de mer, he said.
I went out on other boats after that day,
careful to take something to help me cope
with being out of my element because nothing,
no thing, was more bitter to me than pity.
But today I watched a young woman
rescue a live grasshopper from her puppy
gently convincing him to open his mouth.
It rested a moment then leapt to its new life,
which it owed *(of course)* to the fact that
my friend was just being observant and kind.

The Seas

The view from a top floor flat is far from the coast, the sky its own sea,
rear bedroom window a lookout, mind free as night clouds on the sea.

Backyard roofs and fences are easily waves, street tree tops are flickering
white caps in the wind, crescent sails of a galleon, the moon in an old sea.

Far away, beyond the blue horizon, Norfolk pines rattle creaking masts,
harbour moored in Ashfield Park. Ships rock, now safely home from sea.

Edges fade between sea and sky. Tides roll in, taking over. Mists dim the edge
of horizon reality. Young souls slip to the edge of sleep. Call of a dreaming sea.

Yet I dreamed apart. No pirate flag or treasure chart called me from the window.
I watched and wrote. Tides became lines for poems I sent sailing out to sea.

When I Can Lie Still in Bed No Longer

When I can lie still in bed no longer
I open the window and let a siren in.
Unheard before through double glazing,
it scouts the room like a lost air spirit
then wails its way up the highway
heading towards someone's sorrow.
Not steady, but coming and going.
Intermittent, like a grief's tiring voice.
But because I am up and listening in
I also hear the ducks return to the dam –
the kiss of its surface as they touch down.
The flurry and sweet disquiet of their settling
says they're home safe from their night hunt
and will be serenely here in the morning.

Growing Up with Donald Duck

After years of self-analysis, I'm still unsure as to why I lack a temper.
But it might explain my attraction to Donald Duck and his holy temper.

For he's most things I'm not: manic, vain, selfish, greedy, self-absorbed,
(I did say most things) but that bill-reverberating quack of Donald's temper!

Think of the pantheon of Walt Disney cartoons and comic strip characters,
imprinted like a negative on a child's vacant mind, just one with a temper.

Not Mickey Mr Squeaky-Voice-Fixit, all grin and buttons Big-Ears, never fazed
by danger. Depression-era hero, he wins by his smarts, never with a temper.

But Oh, Donald Fauntleroy Duck. Near unintelligible in his pompous rave,
with top half sailor suit, bow tie, rakish cap, cocky strut exploding a tonne of temper!

And no pants. That white tuft of cheeky tail is a statement salute in itself.
He loves life with a grin, loses heart to begin, then fires up his temper

and wins! Bullies and Beagle Boys, the fickle, unforgiving Finger of Fate,
all fall away before the tsunami torrent of Donald's irrepressible temper.

World War hovered, stage for a nation's choice between Nice Guy and Donald.
I tell my kids. Be silk and steel, velvet in the iron of your temper.

The River

My father always told me, *Love many, trust few*
(there's more) … *always paddle your own canoe.*
Why this was the advice he was drawn to
I do not know, but his mentors were few.
Did the strong rhyme win him, staying in mind
because it was what a bereaved father told
his motherless son, to help make his life
more bearable and navigable than his own?
He was always ahead of me on the river
occasionally glancing back, rarely slowing,
his eyes on the landscape like an explorer.
Now I too am moving fast through water
and sometimes I hear my own children
paddling behind me, my father's daughter.

The Quiet American

He came to her from far away, from across the Pacific, the quiet American.
From jazz, comics, radio, romantic movies and pop culture, a polite American.

Even in uniform, private-corporal, corporal-private, his creams casual, elegant
as a Broadway star, tap dancing across the war to Australia, the right American.

And kind, she could tell, or convinced herself, and he was soft spoken, so unlike
her family's men, who could rip to anger quick as look, but this nice American.

It was passionate, she related, much later. Hard to imagine them in a clinch outside
her sister's home. Cue: *Strings. Moonglow. Closeup.* Cut to a star-bright American.

Part of war in the Pacific, there's a wedding in St Vincent's. She's in her sister's gown,
he's disguised as a soldier. Soon a child makes its way to life, delight for an American.

War moves its pieces across the map of Papua, his snaps not much bigger than stamps.
Goofing with mates as she knits and waits. Japan dissolves in a bright light. Americans.

Every story has a beginning, middle and thread-tying end. The denouement in this case
is protracted. V for someone's victory. Love promises to return. Flight of the American.

The river is wide, says the popular song, *and I cannot cross o'er*, but an ocean is wider.
Like puppets they pull their strings, but snap. She dangles. He falls, a slight American.

Dying herself, my mother, seventy years later, I ask of him again. She still sees Bill,
she says, in dreams. They're both at a dance, but apart. In the twilight, an American.

Tallarook Cemetery

In dreams they come to us, innocently, our dead,
not knowing that they have crossed back over
the ocean that we learnt early on to dread.
Our soldiers and babies, our friends and lovers.
Silent, or speaking in languages we don't know,
they vanish like story book ghosts at first light
and we find ourselves bereft and alone,
forgotten travellers who wake up quayside.
Tallarook cemetery makes death seem simpler.
Headstones have let go of beloved detail.
In the morning light they sing only of love.
The old keeper, pointing to flowers in the grass
unfurling in the unseasonable warmth,
tells us to enjoy the weather while it lasts.

One Breath

For Gwyneth & Cosima

Nine months kept alive by blood from your mother's heart to a breath
of hospital air, the universe alters from inside to out, all in one breath.

Birth came with a tap, one of five senses first to react as they connect
to life outside the womb. Vital signs light up, flashing from one breath.

Your lungs, long dormant, wake perfect pitch, finely tuned as any organ
set for recital. First performance, first composition all sung in one breath.

Your costume is swaddling, ancient as birth itself. Did a wardrobe mistress
wait in the wings, alert for her cue to enter, the first song from one breath?

I write from first photographs as your new grandfather, see my daughter's
soft smile of maternity as you inhale the same air, two breaths in one breath.

Time Waster

My mother loved babies all her long life.
Time waster, you're a time waster, she crooned
to three generations of her descendants
holding each one searchingly up to the light
in hands at first lithe and lightly freckled,
later cramped and crocodiled by age and sun
but always strong enough to lift each sack,
the small belly slumping inside sprigged cotton.
Part accusation, part acclamation.
The song she rocked all her children by.
Time waster. She would have sung it to me,
her youngest, and most troubling child
but only when I was far too young to
understand or misunderstand what it meant.

The Naming of Clouds

For my mother

She remembered the first day of school was *The Naming of Clouds*,
a moment still glimpsed like a sunbeam that came with the clouds.

Later that day there was maypole dancing, sewing and making the dress
she never wore, but her young mind had grown, retaining the clouds.

Other words came from beyond school: speck fruit, bread and dripping,
broken biscuits, strikes, the 'moonlight flits' under a game of clouds.

*We moved so many times between North Belmore & Belmore, Catholic
to Public schools.* No pence for sport? You're shamed, sent under a cloud.

Depression treats: frozen orange thrown at a wall becomes an ice block,
a pie's pastry peeled in exquisite layers is contentment framed by clouds.

Dux of her Class! A troop of nuns march to the flat with magpie intent.
But fourteen means factories for working girls, the sameness of clouds.

Life makes lexicons. Hers include: *war, soldiers, American, wedding, son,
widow, milk bar, shop floor.* Yet good times came with the rain filled clouds.

For there was dancing at the Troc, jiving with friends in dresses patterned
from *Butterick & Vogue.* A girl turns before her mirror in a fantasy cloud.

Her decades deal good hands and bad, played with grace and hope. Cards
from friends and family arrive, one always missing, his remains under clouds.

I am heir to her life, the succour she found in family, music, books and film.
Words gleaned by her resilience made this poem from the naming of clouds.

**In her nineties, my mother enjoyed
dancing classes in her aged care home**

I open my phone and my dead mum dances,
standout on a stage full of old women
being guided by young women in saris.
She moves with unmistakable rhythm.
Hands, shoulders, hips lift and tilt. Her feet glide.
There is a sway that I never saw in real life.
She shrugs, glances, nods, smiles, a princess bride
ready for the drama of being mother and wife.
My best friend had a jewelry box I coveted
because of its tiny captive ballerina
pirouetting even as you lifted the lid.
It was a constancy feat that I loved.
I didn't need to know what drove her,
that sweet face always turning to me.

The Dance

Of remedies of love she knew per chaunce,
For she koude of that art the olde daunce
The Wife of Bath – Geoffrey Chaucer

She koude of that art the olde dance.
Bravo wife, bold in the timeless dance.

Love and dance, metaphor enhanced
as a couple entwined combine in dance.

The young vow to stay in time forever
The old seek time to love and dance.

Ten thousand years ago dancers carved
us on their walls. No change in this dance.

My drug of life, as precious as food, oxygen,
and will to go on, pilgrim in this primal dance.

Today's Best Task

For Tilly

Today's best task is to buy a gift
for a newborn baby. I pass by toys.
A small sage, she needs no fripperies.
I pass by silver cups and Bunnykins bowls.
What I choose is a handmade growsuit
in a floral fabric, a flower meadow
for her belly to breathe life into.
Arbours for her feet. Hedgerows for her limbs.
Like an infant goddess of fertility and love
she will be clothed in roses, marigold and pinks.
And of course, daisies. Day's eye. This is her.
one small human, opening up to the light.
Learning, as we all must, to not fear the dark.
Accepting that, like the sun, it too gives life.

Children of War

Bless all children at the moment of birth, but the child of war
bless more. Think to be born in trauma. Mourn a child of war.

Imagine a sky laced with fire, the earth itself shaken to its core,
new mother crying with fearful joy, her infant defiled by war.

See (but you can't) the father's mind pierced with bullets, shells
yet to hit, his care and longing stifled, his need denied by war.

Friends and family who other times would be gathered close as a host
now scatter like rubble or hide inside it, their love sent wild by war.

My family survived but didn't. A ship took my father an ocean from us
broken. Bless all war born children and children of those who die in war.

Angel

From my perch on the city gate
I watch people go up the cobbled lane
or vanish below me though the portal named
after someone good enough to be called a saint.
But even I, with these stony eyes can see
that of my travellers, some, a few, one
must deserve not sainthood but a, *Well done,*
a virtual pat from humanity.
This man. Old enough to be a child of war.
Ok at being good. At being alive, better.
He salutes the day with his baton of bread
dodges bikes, buys cheese, gathers fresh water.
The bells aim hourly lessons at his head
but they fall harmlessly around him like rain.

Portal

i.m.

He was *working on his soul,* he said, as he began to leave the portal
of life, fading from his hospital bed towards another, distant portal.

He was one of us, ones who see the world somewhat askance
through words, that fusion of thought and feeling, a poets' portal.

There, moons swing like coins on the sun's necklace, the spheres' music
calls to souls, meteorites shower a violet light, star path to the last portal.

Carpe diem. Yet how many days can a life hold before the hands atrophy?
The mind returns looking for clues, celestial detective casing a star's portal.

Even the word emerges like a ghostly shape trying to find itself: *gate,*
passage, refuge, port, a place where ships may shelter from storms: portal.

Each friend's death diminishes and enhances us. We grow with the loss,
join his ship sheltering in stars, before he sails alone to a waiting portal.

John and Jo

When thoughts of inconstancy bother me
I think of you, John Keats, wasting in Rome
in a small room, the city at your window
exquisitely alive and noisy,
and of your friend, Jo Severn there
with his *warm and capable* hands, to feed you,
to clean you, to tend the fire, to sketch you
one last time, recording the sweat in your hair,
and at your request, checking the cemetery
where you (and years later, he) would be laid,
reporting back to you the white daisies
growing up around the gravestones,
(as they still do today) taking their moment
beneath our blue, inexplicable sky.

Ms Death

Summer in Rome. Crowd confetti with gelato, plazas packed to death.
Tourists transit from one world to another and, slouched on a step, Death.

Heat hovers, making a mirage of the square. Crucifixes line the Seven Hills.
Faces glow with holiday hope. But one fades to white, an afterglow of death.

Eternity in each eye, greased skull and cheeks, straight line lips painted black.
A hoodie hangs on skinny jeans and Doc Martens, a skeleton bored to death.

The scythe might be a broomstick from another time. Black plastic tape flutters
danger from its blade. Yet something surreal suggests she's the real deal, Ms Death.

A cardboard coffin wobbles lightly on its stand above a white, polystyrene cup,
her ironic nod to life. She drains a last fag, more Death-warmed-up than Death.

Standing, she searches sentinel across the plaza, looking for likely souls, anyone
cruising on the edge of the cosmos feigning invisibility (or invincibility) from death.

No John Keats, but still a poet sick in Rome, teetering on the edge of breakdown
between Vatican and Colosseum, mind typing SOS, I blink and back winks Death.

It's a sudden sense of looking into life's last black hole, outer space becoming inner
without the star trek, then the familiarity of going home to comfort and rest in death.

But I break my eyes, feel my life snap and rock as the cortisone kicks. There are beads
to buy for luck, scenes to see of someone's idea of heaven, and a god nailed to death.

On Being Human

Joyous dogs in the Borghese Gardens
are innocent of art, religion, philosophy.
They lollop away from owners, enchanted
by bird droppings and other dogs' shit.
In the gallery, Bernini's Daphne,
half-human-half-tree, is forever caught
within, forever eluding, Apollo's grasp.
Under our four-century long gaze
her fingers are turning to leafy twigs
her toes to roots, her marble flesh to bark.
Not for her the heartache and natural shocks
that we are heir to. It is time to go home.
Dogs and humans converge at the gates
as the city lights itself up in the dusk.

The Sky Inside

i.m.

The myth of Daphne is far removed from Joanna, of *The Sky Inside,*
her journal of work and love and way of looking at the sky, inside.

She is no dweller in Acadia by the river Ladon, no god pursued her
egged on by Cupid's curse, but her forever love lives in the sky inside.

Not the quick clutch of lust which masquerades as love, theirs ran river
deep, years flowing like a constant stream, like stars, like the sky inside.

He was maker, she dancer, in their house of wood, music and light, nights
and days the only sense of time beneath the cosmos of their sky inside.

But cancer has no sense of time. It simply is, entering like a kind of fate
unearned, undeserved. Life-like it grows in us but never in the sky inside.

In the aftermath, she continues, sustained by loving memory and grace.
The light of lost love grows within her now, sunlight on the sky inside.

Phantom Pain

Of all the questions that I never asked
my first world war veteran grandfather
and his double amputee younger brother
it's the one about phantom pain that haunts me.
I was held back by my sense of the irony
(and the rudeness) of asking about pain
in something that was no longer there.
I grew up. Life supplied approximations.
Like what it's like to miss something you thought
you would have. Lost futures close as words
whited out. Milestones missed. Grief.
Still, what was it like for those young men
to dream of playing footy or digging their toes
into the sand at St Kilda, and then wake up?

Reflection in London

There are three photographs of him, images in a window in London,
roads wet in the square, passers-by somewhere anywhere in London.

He doesn't hide the camera phone, although it becomes quite invisible
in the flash of making an image of a man waving at nothing in London.

There must have been a gap or two between shots since the red van left
stage left and a new set of strangers bent under a summer shower in London.

Everyone is purposeful, jackets and hair blown as they stride this morning
to work, an engagement or headed for home. He might be alone in London.

No one notices him raising a phone before his face like a shield, or a pass
to enter something waiting to happen in another time and place in London.

Behind the man, but facing the window reflection, taxis and other traffic nudge
themselves. There's bunting across the street, sign of a mystery play in London.

Slim and athletic, sports top and vest projecting indifference to weather, expression
expressionless, he's focused on the task of a moment, to be moments ago in London.

In Stockholm, Oslo and once at a play in Melbourne, I took similar photographs, front
and centre of life as a landscape in time rushed by, a living statue there and in London.

Hidden Self Portraits

Some, not a lot, did it – hid their own self portrait
in others' commissioned portraits,
or in biblical, classical or historical scenes,
casting themselves as worshipper, courtier, soldier.
In his Last Judgement, Michelangelo cast himself
between Christ and the damned man. He is Bartholomew
flayed alive, a slack mantle of human skin. A joke
directed at critics or a personal statement, or both.
Others presented themselves as reflections,
in a mirror or windowpane. But Clara Peeters,
looks at us from lids of stoneware jugs
or raised parts of goblets, a woman 'caught'
as a detail in the 'now' of her still lifes
her quiet "I was here" to the rushing universe.

Self Portrait at Sixteen with Jack Kerouac

The night you leave your suburb behind you is like leaving fifteen for sixteen.
Stairs from subways rise to the tornado of Emerald City. Red sneakers at sixteen.

Friday night could be Christmas or New Year. Traffic lines jam intersections, head-
-lights roam the crowd of nightwalkers. Light and dark is about to start at sixteen.

Each pub is its own theatre, three act plays in every corner. Cracked cream-green
tiles awash with beer stream with teenage certainty, vomit and blood at sixteen.

Too young to drink legal, the illegal thrill rises like bubbles on heads of beer
and you. Light as a balloon inflated by being half-boy, you fly high at sixteen.

Williams Street climbs to invade Kings Cross, its neon horizon of adulthood
collision of worlds. Calvary waits as you bear the rough cross of being sixteen.

Jack Kerouac trudges ahead in jeans and chequered shirt from the *Dharma Bums*.
Acolyte, you follow his trail of jazz and poems with the desolation of being sixteen.

The night ends with a week's pocket money gone in a taxi. You wake to a chorus
of lawnmowers. Yet how beatific to feel beat, just shy of being beautiful. At sixteen.

Everyone Tells You

Everyone tells you it is too dangerous to hitchhike.
But when you are fifteen, you do it anyway.
Cut your teeth with friendly surfers and farmers
on your island home where all roads lead to the beach.
Two years later in forest country, a whispering man
in a porkpie hat keeps driving towards the sheer drop.
Winged seeds fly in the windows. You leap out
at a petrol station and are picked up by young men
who drive far inland to show you their work camp.
You smile and keep a hand on your souvenir penknife.
Nothing happens. They drop you in a tourist town.
But now your arms are too heavy to lift in goodbye,
your fingers too brittle to wave. Your long hair sparks
like kindling in the cold air. Your shadow is unfamiliar.

"Afoot and light-hearted I take to the open road"

Walt Whitman, Song of the Open Road

Afoot, my friend Dave and I tramp across rivers and Singapore bridges, hitching to far Penang. We raise shy thumbs, happy to breathe pre Lee Kwan Yew sewerage on *The Road to Penang.*

Light-hearted? Yes, light as two twenty year old friends can be in early 1965. We've skipped war in Vietnam under cover of being on-leave public servants to test our manhood hitching to Penang.

Across the causeway and strait into Malaysia we rucksack, quite careless of the traffic phalanx, its early cacophony, thrilling to first time sights, sounds and smells, bound north for far Penang.

Somewhere on the nearby coast is Changi, a name clanging like prison bars from POW stories. Stoic soldiers inform and strengthen our adventure as we risk rides merely to reach Penang.

There must have been lifts, for we are open-faced and innocent, green as a tropical summer. Our years shine like fresh spray from a wave rolling the Pacific all the way north to far Penang.

The rides come, constant as curiosity. Our drug of preference is being alive, thrilling to the exotic. Each temple, house, roadside stall or gathering is cornucopia for senses striving to reach Penang.

Colour riots with the aroma of incense in Malacca. Pretty pink and white buildings from Portuguese in peaceful city squares. Powerful curries and gun shots at night produce curious smiles. To Penang!

K.L. and the heat equatorial. We stand alert as statues in sunglasses, dripping sweat. Rides rumble into traffic past playing fields and mosques majestic. We rake into the city, a day's hitch to Penang.

Arrival! But now my bosom companion Dave from Barrow and I will part. He will hitch his way unbroken across the half-world. My way to see other friends globe-dotted, leads from Penang.

South, ever south, shining new seven league boots survive a solo road to Singapore, then ship for Hong Kong, hard class sleeper to Beijing, Ulan Bator, Moscow and Helsinki, far from Penang.

Afoot, alone but hope-hearted, I hitch from Helsinki to Stockholm to Oslo. A Sydney stripling hails Vikings on Independence Day, 17th May. Cars hurry to host me a hostel far from Penang!

A lifetime of travel trails into the ether of Eternity. Lucky to carry the confidence trick of being a boy, lucky to make man. Our risk in the sixties was death, worse, our sisters' Road to Penang.

The Ginkgo in the Mine

Because I am ill and would like to be cured,
a concept learnt years ago and hard to forget,
I accept the Chinese medicine practitioner's
questions, quivering steel probes and herbs.
She is trying to get something flowing again.
My paper bag of quills, shavings, seeds and flakes
smells like an old forest of living and felled trees.
Yet I am disappointed that Ginkgo, the living fossil,
and renowned cure-all, is not included.
My favourite 'exotic' tree since early childhood,
I love its pretty fans and how as a temple tree
it withstood the Hiroshima bombing.
Here, Wonthaggi miners found Ginkgo fossils
while blasting for fuel to keep us alight.

Acorn

The backyard was littered with bullet snubs of acorns
fired by an upstairs parent, the tree we called an 'acorn'.

Innocent inner city renters, no biology know-how
breached the backyard mystery of the exotic acorn.

And it was young then, slouched against the fence,
an adolescent clicking for attention. *Lookit me, A.Corn.*

But softer, its *cup shaped cupule of indurated bracts*
were sweet gumnut babies in a nursery acorn.

Wars still thrived in the backyard since war fared
everywhere. *Ammo* was a cache of stockpiled acorn.

In time, of course, it became a sailing ship, just once
a mountain, prone to avalanche with falling acorns.

But as ship full sail, breasting a gale-howling Southerly,
it's best remembered, cockpit sheering clouds of acorns.

Branches bent to the wind, veering over the neighbours
into Eternity. I hung on howling in the thrash of acorns.

The oak it was eventually, never stayed true to memory.
Oaks are another story. In Sherwood. Ours was an Acorn.

Suburban Laboratory

For Jack, who kept Coca-Cola for cleaning

My father grew crystals in our garage,
Sulphur, Borax, Copper Sulphate, Alum,
for the beauty in their ordered growth.
He marked up seashells and sea urchins
gathered on our annual beach holidays,
to demonstrate the Fibonacci sequence.
He reassembled the pet cat's skeleton
to help explain its ability to climb.
From a twist of leaves in a tin can
he grew a tree that I loved to dream in.
When Dad had to cut it down years later,
I feigned indifference until he gave me
trunk slices he'd kept so that I could admire
their secret record of our time; tree rings

Racing

In the backyard of a flat a boy carves out a track for racing.
Small, coloured plastic cars are all he has to begin racing.

He pulls up cape weed, buffalo grass and dandelion, makes
a circle of dirt beneath the clothesline for invisible racing.

Invisible to adults. Women walk to and fro from the laundry
inside the copper's steam, mind on washing, blind to racing.

At track-squint level pebbles are boulders, grass stalks
make a wood. He hand rakes the track each time for racing.

The cars are plastic, thumb long, moulded with no wheels
in primary colours. They're pushed and flicked to start racing.

One push-flick can never be just the same as another. Some
slew, others skim ahead to avoid crashes while they're racing.

Winning is important for blue and green, his favourite colours,
(so they do) but it's the patterns he looks to most while racing.

Crouched, his camera eyes record above and trackside views.
Light touch adjusts aesthetic of race, shape and order of racing.

Solitary but mind-accompanied, a creative imagination grows
from car-play to word-touch to poems, my child's mind racing.

The Game

Ubi sunt qui ante nos in mundo fuere?

When summer's ferocity abated
and our backyard began to smell of rain
we children played with our matchbox cars
in towns we'd carefully conjure in the dirt
but later flood behind our father's back
with tides of the still rationed tank water
–afraid to provoke his righteous anger
at the waste and at our terrible glee.
Now, we are just old siblings, at a life stage
in which we take no pleasure in destruction
and no refuge in the plea of innocence.
We miss the old man with the stern voice
calling us in from the yard, telling us
to do something better with our time.

About the Authors

Ross Donlon

Ross Donlon is winner of two international poetry prizes and the Launceston Cup, premier spoken word event of the Tasmanian Poetry Festival. Other awards include the Varuna Dorothy Hewett Flagship Fellowship. He has five books of poems published (including *Sjovegen - The Sea Road* - translated into Norwegian) - and is co author of *Kickstarting Poetry Books 1&2* (Blake) with Tric O'Heare. Widely published in Australia and also in the U.K. and Ireland, he has featured at various poetry festivals and events in Australia. He is represented in numerous anthologies both in Australia and the UK. and has read his work at festivals in Ireland, England and Scotland as well as readings in Norway, Poland and Romania. He is also convenor of Poetry from Agitation Hill and is publisher of Mark Time Books.

Tric O'Heare

Tric O'Heare's poetry has appeared in many Australian journals, newspapers and anthologies. Her first poetry collection, *Tender Hammers*, was published by Five Islands Press in 2003, and the chap book, *Fear of Umbrellas* by Mark Time Books in 2013. Her collection *Marrow* (Mark Time Books, 2021) gathers work written over twenty years and *Like a Girl on a Page* (Mark Time Books, 2024) is a recent collection focused on one life-changing tragedy. She has had poems shortlisted or commended in international competitions including the ACU Poetry Prize 2020, 2021 and 2024 and the Newcastle Poetry Prize 2012, and won two national competitions. O'Heare co-authored with Ross Donlon two books on teaching poetry, *Kickstarting Poetry 1* and 2, (Blake Education, 2005).